LANTZ

I Can Read About

EARTHQUAKES AND VOLCANOES

Written by Deborah Merrians
Illustrated by Greg Harris

Troll Associates

Illustrations copyright © 1996 by Greg Harris.

Text copyright © 1996 by Troll Communications L. L. C.

Published by Troll Associates, an imprint and registered trademark of Troll Communications L. L. C.

Printed in the United States of America.

10 9 8 7 6 5 4 3 2 1

Library of Congress Cataloging-in-Publication Data
Merrians, Deborah.
    I can read about earthquakes and volcanoes / written by Deborah Merrians ; illustrated by Greg Harris.
    p. cm.
    ISBN 0-8167-3648-0 (lib. bdg.). — ISBN 0-8167-3649-9 (pbk.)
    1. Earthquakes—Juvenile literature.   2. Volcanoes—Juvenile
literature.   [1. Earthquakes.   2. Volcanoes.]   I. Harris,   Greg, (Date)   ill. II. Title.
QE521.3.M47 1995
551.2'2—dc20   95-5944

One sunny day, some years ago, in a village in Mexico, a farmer was busily plowing his field. Suddenly, the sky became very dark and still.

A loud rumbling noise came from
under the earth. The soil under
the farmer's feet got very hot,
and the ground began to
shake and tremble.

As the farmer ran for safety, a loud explosion ripped through the earth, shooting rocks into the sky. It formed a mountain over one hundred feet (30.4 meters) high.

Smoke, ashes, and hot, flowing rock called *lava* shot out of the mountain. The farmer was watching a volcano being born! In time, the volcano would grow to a thousand feet (304 meters) in height.

Volcanoes and the trembling forces in the ground called earthquakes happen all the time. They are part of nature and begin far below the earth's surface.

If you could cut open the earth you would see many layers.

crust
5-25 miles
(8-40 kilometers) wide

mantle
1,800 miles
(3,000 kilometers) wide

outer core
1,400 miles
(2,250 kilometers) wide

inner core
800 miles
(1,300 kilometers) wide

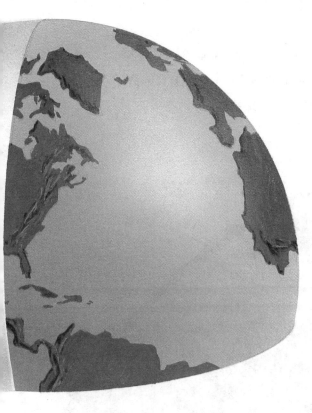

The outside layer is called the *crust*. It is anywhere from 5 to 25 miles (8 to 40 kilometers) thick. In terms of the earth, the crust is really a thin layer. The crust is covered with mountains, rivers, trees, water, soil, and rocks.

Next comes the *mantle*. Although it is solid, it does contain melted rock, called *magma*.

Then comes the *outer core*, which is made up of liquid rock. At the center is the *inner core*, which scientists believe is either solid or a huge crystal made of iron.

The mantle is below the crust of the earth. It is 1,800 miles (3,000 kilometers) wide and contains rock material and magma. Hot liquid magma also contains gas and steam.

crust

mantle

It is very, very hot beneath the earth's surface. Under the earth—10 to 40 miles (16 to 64 kilometers) beneath the surface—hot magma and gasses collect in pools.

There is also great pressure beneath the earth's surface.

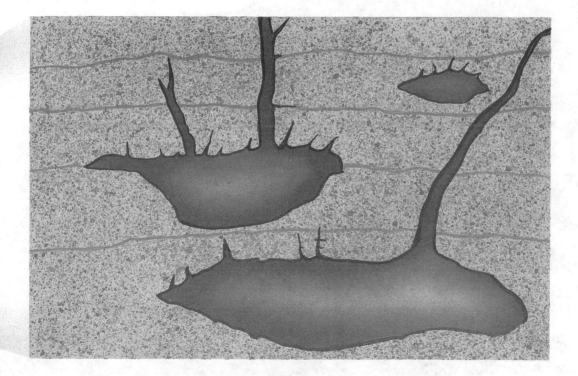

When there is a weak spot on the earth's surface, the pressure can cause the magma to push up to the top.

mantle

magma

When this happens—
when great pressure forces
magma to break through
the crust of the earth—a
volcano is born.

When magma pushes out of the crust of the earth, it is called lava. Some lava oozes gently out of the earth. Some lava pours out. Other times, lava erupts violently from the earth. It shoots up and out, along with ashes, gasses, and steam.

A volcano erupts somewhat like soda in a bottle. If you shake an open bottle of warm soda . . . whoosh!

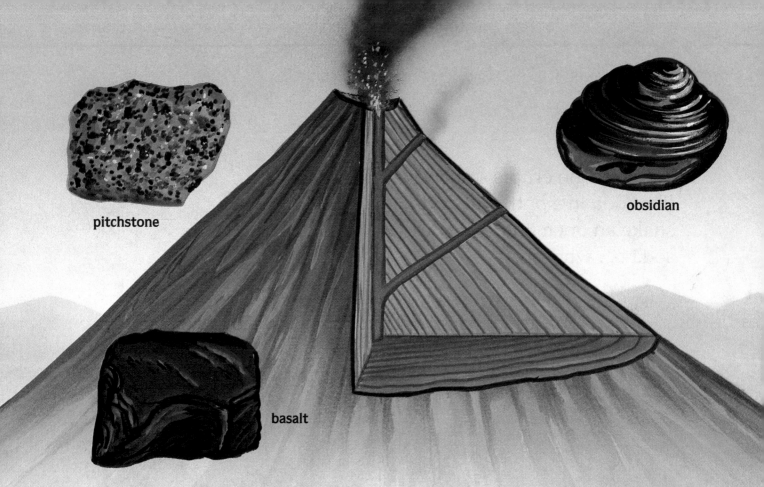

pitchstone

obsidian

basalt

A volcano may keep erupting lava for many years. Lava running down the sides of a volcano will eventually cool and harden into rock called *igneous* (IG-ne-us) rock. In time, the volcano will look like a cone-shaped mountain.

An erupting volcano is a sight to behold. Fiery plumes of lava explode above the volcano's rim, shooting hundreds of feet into the air. It is like watching nature's very own show of fireworks.

Long ago, people did not know that the forces of nature caused volcanoes and earthquakes. They were frightened by the mysterious rumblings under the earth's surface.

Some people believed that the earth was like a large, upside-down bowl. The bowl was held up by two elephants standing on the back of a turtle. When the earth trembled, people thought that the elephants were moving.

The ancient Romans thought that Vulcan, the god of fire, had his shop under an island off the coast of Italy. When Vulcan worked, his pounding hammer made the earth shake. The fires from his furnace sent smoke and ashes out of the mountains.

Other people thought that the trembling of the earth was caused by giant whales slapping their tails against the floor of the ocean.

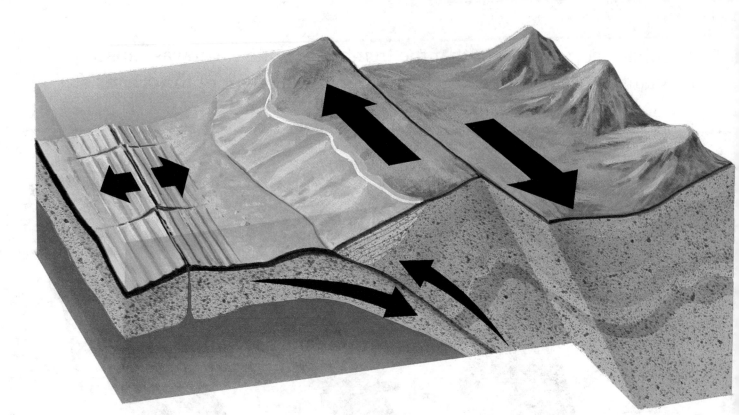

Today, we have different ideas, or theories.

Scientists now believe that the continents and oceans of the world do not stay still. They move or drift slightly. There are at least seven huge plates underneath the crust of the earth. The continents and oceans rest on top of these plates. These huge plates are between the crust and the mantle of the earth.

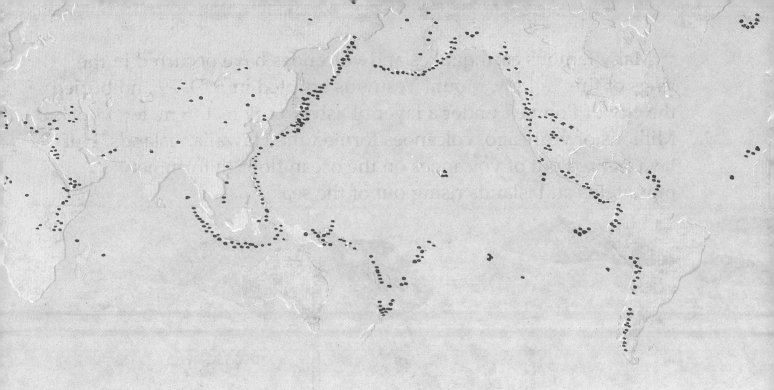

Earthquakes and volcanoes seem to happen most often in the places where these huge plates touch or bump into each other. Earthquakes and volcanoes seem to start in weak parts of the earth's crust.

Scientists can map most of the areas in the world where volcanoes have erupted and where they may strike again. These areas are called rings of fire.

Many famous earthquakes and volcanoes have occurred in the rings of fire. In Italy, Mount Vesuvius erupted in A.D. 79 and buried the city of Pompeii under a layer of ash twenty feet (6 meters) thick. Millions of years ago, volcanoes formed the Hawaiian islands. Hot lava poured out of volcanoes on the ocean floor to form new mountains and islands rising out of the sea.

An earthquake happens when the crust of the earth cracks, making the crust shift and shake. The San Andreas fault in California is a large crack in the earth's crust. In 1906, it helped cause the San Francisco earthquake. Today scientists study this active fault to try to find a way to predict when earthquakes will occur.

Long ago, there was no way of telling when an earthquake or volcano would strike, and many people died. Today scientists can sometimes predict when an earthquake may happen or when a volcano might erupt. They use special devices that send out laser beams to monitor movements in the earth's plates and fault lines.

A seismograph (SIZ-ma-graf) is an instrument used to record the power of an earthquake. A simple seismograph has a pen hanging over a piece of paper. As the earth trembles, the pen records vibrations and makes lines on the paper. If the earthquake is getting stronger, the marks on the paper get longer.

Some earthquakes are so small they only shake the ground
as much as a heavy truck on a quiet city street.

Other earthquakes are so big, they can cause entire mountains to fall into the cracks in the earth.

Some earthquakes take place under the sea. Cracking can occur on the ocean floor. When the crust slips on the bottom of the ocean floor, it can cause the start of a big wave. The Japanese word for this kind of wave is tsunami (su-NAHM-e). If the big wave reaches land, it can wreck everything in its path.

Scientists are always on the alert for earthquakes. Whether the earthquake is large or small, a seismograph in New York can record the shock waves from an earthquake thousands of miles away.

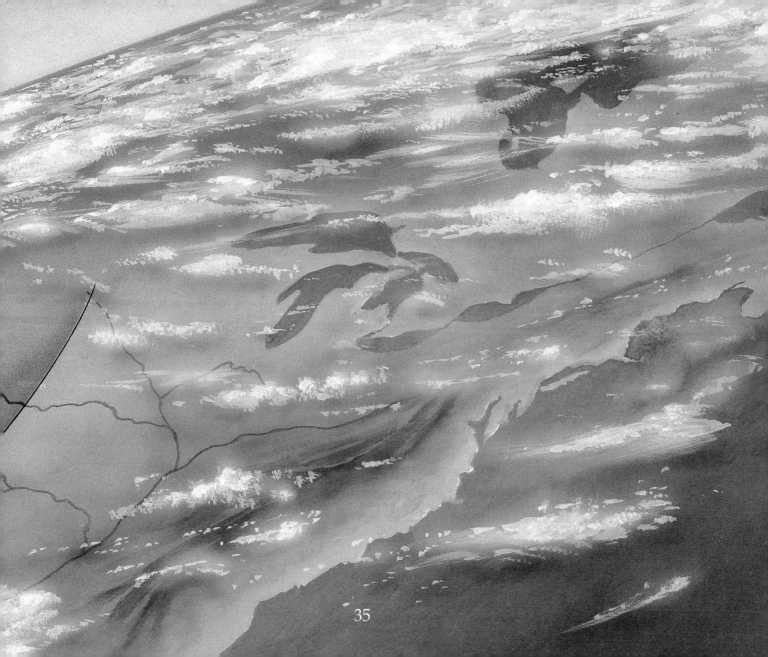

Scientists are always studying volcanoes, too. They use special tools to find out what lava is made of and how hot it gets. Photographs and radar images of volcanoes taken from space are also helpful to scientists. They use these images to study how volcanoes affect our weather.

For many people in the world, living in the shadow of a volcanic mountain is a way of life.

In spite of the damage that earthquakes and volcanoes cause, many people return to the land to rebuild their homes.

Many of the people make good use of
the grassy slopes of a volcanic mountain. The soil,
a mixture of earth and lava, is very good for farming.

In Hawaii, the volcanoes are a tourist attraction. One of these volcanoes, Mauna Loa, erupted in 1984. The gas and steam from the eruption created a cloud over seven miles (11 kilometers) high. The lava flow from the erupting volcano covered over 18 square miles (29 square kilometers).

Hawaii

In other parts of the world, steam from volcanoes is used to heat water and to generate electricity.

Some scientists believe that heated water from under the earth may someday provide us with a rich source of energy.

Scientists study land volcanoes such as Mount Saint Helens and the great mountain ranges below the sea to try and learn more about our changing earth.

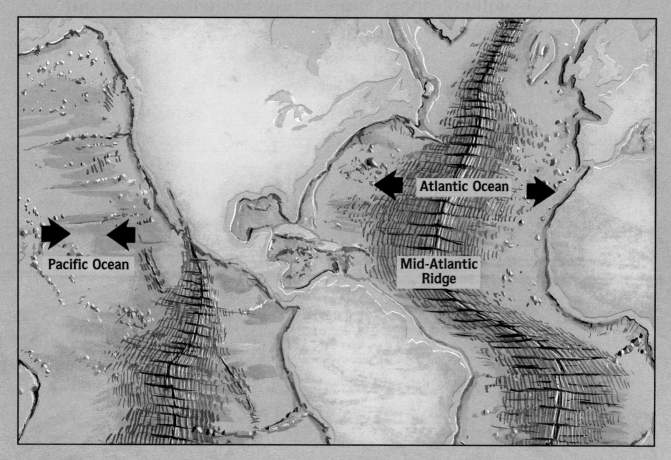

Is magma oozing at the bottom of the Atlantic Ocean and helping to widen the ocean? Is the Pacific Ocean getting narrower? Scientists think so. We still have so much to learn.

What secrets will volcanoes and earthquakes tell us about our mysterious and changing earth?